WITHDRAWN
TORBAY LIBRARIES

14 SEP 2011

40p

TQ

South Korea

Fred Martin

First published in Great Britain by Heinemann Library
Halley Court, Jordan Hill, Oxford OX2 8EJ
a division of Reed Educational and Professional Publishing Ltd

Heinemann is a registered trademark of Reed Educational and Professional Publishing Ltd

OXFORD FLORENCE PRAGUE MADRID ATHENS
MELBOURNE AUCKLAND KUALA LUMPUR SINGAPORE TOKYO
IBADAN NAIROBI KAMPALA JOHANNESBURG GABORONE
PORTSMOUTH NH (USA) CHICAGO MEXICO CITY SAO PAULO

© Reed Educational and Professional Publishing Ltd 1998

The moral right of the proprietor has been asserted.

All rights reserved. No part of this publication may be reproduced, stored in a retrieval system, or transmitted in any form or by any means, electronic, mechanical, photocopying, recording, or otherwise without either the prior written permission of the Publishers or a licence permitting restricted copying in the United Kingdom issued by the Copyright Licensing Agency Ltd, 90 Tottenham Court Road, London W1P 9HE.

Designed by AMR
Illustrations by Art Construction
Printed in Hong Kong / China

02 01 00 99 98
10 9 8 7 6 5 4 3 2 1

ISBN 0 431 01371 3

British Library Cataloguing in Publication Data
Martin, Fred, 1948-
 South Korea. – (Next Stop)
 1. Korea (South) – Geography – Juvenile literature
 I.Title
 915.1'95

Acknowledgements
The Publishers would like to thank the following for permission to reproduce photographs:
Aspect Pictures, J. Alex Langley, p.14; Colorific Photo Library, Kari Ahlberg/Lehtikuva Oy, p.27 Martti Kainulainen/Lehtikuva Oy, p.22, John Nordell/JB Pictures, p.28, Michael Yamashita, pp.18, 19, 24, 25; Hutchison Library, Michael Macintyre, p.20, Andrew Sole, pp.6, 15; Panos Pictures, Jim Holmes, pp.5, 7, 8, 23; Trip Photo Library, T. Bognor, p.29, R. Nichols, p.10, Trip, pp.4, 9, 11, 12, 13, 16, 17, 21, 26

Cover photographs: Link Picture Library and Gareth Boden

Every effort has been made to contact holders of any material reproduced in this book. Any omissions will be rectified in subsequent printings if notice is given to the Publisher.

CONTENTS

Introduction to South Korea	4
The natural landscape	6
Climate, vegetation and wildlife	8
Towns and cities	10
A city family	12
Farming and fishing	14
A fishing family	16
Markets and shops	18
Food	20
Made in South Korea	22
Transport	24
Arts, leisure and sport	26
Customs and festivals	28
South Korea factfile	30
Glossary	31
Index	32

INTRODUCTION TO SOUTH KOREA

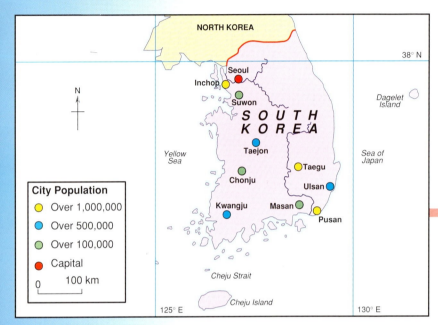

South Korea: towns and population.

The Toksugung Palace in Seoul.
- *Ancient buildings sit side by side with modern skyscrapers in this fast-growing city.*
- *People in South Korea have a very strong sense of their own history.*

Two countries

South Korea and North Korea are two different countries. However North Korea and South Korea share more than just a name. The people in both countries also share the same language, culture and ancient history. Their more recent history has been very different, and this is because of the way they are governed. In North Korea, there is a **communist** government. In South Korea, the country is run as a **capitalist democracy**.

War and division

Korea was invaded and occupied by Japan during World War II. The Russian army recaptured the north and the American army recaptured the south. In 1948, a boundary line was drawn along the 38th parallel of latitude to divide Korea in two: North Korea and South Korea.

Children in South Korea.
- They are celebrating South Korea's independence day.
- They are waving the South Korean flag with its ancient symbol of yin and yang.

In 1950, war broke out between North Korea and South Korea. Scenes in the television series *MASH* show conditions in an American army field hospital during the Korean War. When the war ended, Korea was still divided. There is a **demilitarized zone (DMZ)** between the two countries with border guards always on the alert. In 1996, a North Korean submarine sailed into South Korean waters. There was shooting in which most of the North Korean sailors were killed.

Unfriendly relations

While North Korea is still an **economically developing country**, which means that it is one of the poorest in the world, many people in South Korea have become wealthy. Goods made in South Korea are **exported** all over the world. South Korea's economic success has come about mainly because South Koreans believe that they can do most things better than anyone else, and they are prepared to work hard to prove it.

In 1997, there was a crop failure in North Korea and people were starving. The South Korean government refused to give aid. They said that they did not want to spend money on a country that makes and buys weapons that could be used against them. However, despite their present disagreements, North Korea and South Korea may come together in the future and be one country again.

South Korea's flag is a divided circle on a white background, with some black symbols. The divided circle is an ancient *Confucian* symbol of opposites called yin and yang. Yin shows the negative things in nature. Yang shows the positive things. The patterns of black lines are also ancient symbols.

THE NATURAL LANDSCAPE

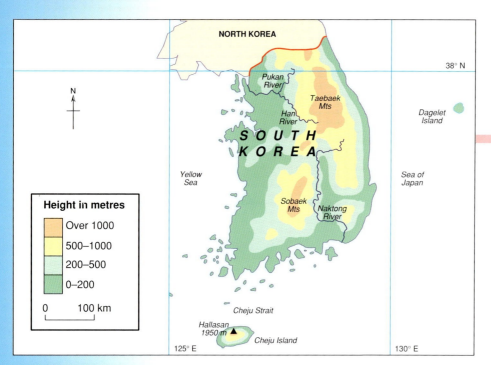

South Korea: natural features.

The Korean peninsula

South Korea is at the southern end of a 960 km **peninsula** that juts out from the eastern side of the continent of Asia. It lies between the Sea of Japan and the Yellow Sea. The total length of the coastline is 2413 km. There are about 3000 small islands close to the peninsula. The largest of these is Cheju Island which is separated from the mainland by the Cheju Strait.

The east coast curves slightly, and does not have many bays or inlets. The south and west coasts are quite different. They have hundreds of long and winding inlets with rocky offshore islands. An unusual feature on the west coast is the big difference in height between high and low tides. This difference, called the **tidal range,** is about nine metres. It is one of the world's largest tidal ranges.

The Ssang-chon river.
- *This river flows through the Sorak Mountains.*
- *The relief of much of South Korea is mountainous.*

The mountain backbone

About 70 per cent of South Korea is mountainous. The Taebaek mountain range stretches like a backbone down the eastern side of the country with the highest peaks reaching about 1500 m. The mountains drop steeply towards the Sea of Japan, giving a rocky coastline with cliffs.

The country's highest mountain is the 1950 m peak of Hallasan on Cheju Island. This whole island is made of flows of lava and other volcanic materials. There are also earthquakes in this part of South Korea. This is because Cheju Island is above a part of the earth's crust where two of the earth's **plates** are moving towards each other. The ground shudders as the Pacific plate slowly slides under the Asian plate. Hot volcanic rocks sometimes come to the surface through cracks in the plates.

The South Korean's own name for their country is Han. This is the same as the name of their longest river.

Rivers and lowland

The **sources** of the main rivers in South Korea are in the Taebaek mountains. From there they then flow west or south. The Han and Pukan rivers join up before flowing into the sea near Seoul. The Nantkong river flows west at first, then south to flow into the Korea Strait at Pusan. The largest areas of lowland are in the river valleys and the coastal plains in the west.

A fishing boat at low tide.
- *There is a big difference between high and low tide.*
- *There are many inlets and islands along the west coast.*

CLIMATE, VEGETATION AND WILDLIFE

The four seasons

The climate of South Korea has four seasons. The coldest season is winter when icy winds blow down from Siberia. The average December temperature in Seoul is –5 °C. By June, the **monsoon** winds have changed direction and blow up from the south. This raises the temperature to an average of 25 °C in Seoul.

Because air from the south picks up water from the seas and the Pacific Ocean, it is much wetter than the air from Siberia. The total amount of rain that falls on Seoul each year is about 1000 mm. Of this, over 350 mm fall in June, with another 200 mm in July.

The spring and autumn seasons are times of change, as the weather varies between the summer and winter extremes. In late summer to autumn, **typhoons** sometimes reach South Korea from the south. Their strong winds and powerful waves can smash fishing boats and buildings.

Plants and wildlife

About 65 per cent of South Korea is forest, though most of the natural woodland has been cleared. The valley bottoms and some of the steep valley sides are now mainly used for farming. Most of the forest consists of broadleaf deciduous trees, though there are also coniferous trees where it is colder. Some areas of attractive landscape are now conserved as national parks. One example is the Kayasan National Park in the south east.

The winter is very cold in most of South Korea.
- *The surface of this lake on the Pukan river has frozen.*
- *Fishing is a popular pastime.*

The Mount Sorak National Park.
- *A forest of deciduous trees with some coniferous trees.*
- *Some natural vegetation and wildlife is conserved in South Korea's national parks.*

There are many types of colourful sub-tropical flowers. The mugunghwa comes into flower all over South Korea between June and October. It is also known as the Rose of Sharon. The Korean name for the flower means 'immortality'. The mugunghwa is a national flower of the country.

There are few large animals left living in the wild. Animals that are **native** to the area such as boar, lynx, tiger, bear and deer are now rare. One animal that is special to South Koreans is the Chindot-kae dog. Most of the dogs are yellow or white, with a thick tail that is rolled up. They are hunting dogs with many features that South Koreans think are important such as loyalty and bravery.

The Chindot-kae dog is so important that it has been named as a national symbol for South Korea. It is also protected under a Cultural Property Protection law.

TOWNS AND CITIES

Capitals old and new

About 1000 years ago, Kyongju in South Korea was one of the world's biggest cities. It was the **capital city** of the ancient Shilla **dynasty**. The remains of temples, tombs and royal buildings are still there. The present population of Kyongju is 142,000.

Seoul was chosen as a capital city about 550 years ago. It is now the capital city of South Korea. There are many high mountains in and around Seoul. The site was believed to have a good *myongdang*. This is the Korean word for the natural energy that helps people who live there.

The city has a long and ancient history with palaces that date back to the Chosun dynasty in the fourteenth century. The Kyongbok palace is the oldest of these. It was first built in 1395 though it has been rebuilt several times since then, most recently in 1995.

Seoul, the capital of South Korea.
- *Seoul is surrounded on three sides by the Pugaksan (turtle), Naksan (blue dragon) and Mallidongsan (white tiger) mountains.*
- *The city is built in valleys formed by the Hangang and Chonggyech'on rivers.*
- *Some people believe that this site gives the city a special energy.*

Modern Seoul

About 30 years ago, Seoul was classed as a **third world** city where most people had a poor standard of living. Now there are modern skyscrapers, hotels, shops, offices and factories. There is a **metro** system to help people get about more easily. The Daehan Life Insurance (DLI) building is the tallest in South Korea, with 63 storeys.

A problem is that some of the buildings were built too quickly. In 1995 a department store collapsed, killing many of the people inside. Soon afterwards, one report said that only two per cent of new high-rise buildings met government safety standards and that fourteen per cent were unsafe.

South Korea's other cities

There are 40 cities in South Korea that have populations of more than 100,000. Pusan on the south coast is the country's second biggest city, with just under four million people. It gets its name from a Korean word meaning 'pot' because it used to be shaped like a big pot. Now Pusan is the country's main sea port. South Korea has become rich mainly by **exporting** goods to other countries. **Raw materials** are also **imported** through Pusan as South Korea has few of its own raw materials.

There are many other smaller towns and cities throughout South Korea, both inland and on the coast. The biggest are centres for commerce, industry and administration. Smaller towns serve as **market towns** for farmers in the surrounding countryside.

Modern Seoul.
- *There are department stores and other modern buildings in Seoul and in South Korea's other cities.*
- *There are good bus services in Seoul.*

Thirty years ago, Ulsan was a small fishing port and local market town. Now it is a city with almost 70,000 people and some of South Korea's biggest shipyards.

A CITY FAMILY

Life in a suburb

Mr and Mrs Shin live in Yangchung-gu, a suburb on the edge of Seoul. Mr Shin's name is Dong-woo and Mrs Shin's name is Ye Byong-sook. They have two boys called Yongsu who is eleven years old, and Yongsok who is eight years old.

The area they live in was built about ten years ago. Almost everyone in the district lives in tall apartment blocks. There are open areas with flowers and trees around each of the blocks. There is also a baseball field, tennis courts and an ice-skating rink nearby.

The Shin's apartment is on the fourth floor of the block. Their apartment has three bedrooms, a living room, kitchen and bathroom.

A day at work

Mr Shin Dong-woo has a busy day. He has an important job with the Hyundai Motor Company which makes cars and other types of vehicles. He gets up at 5.00 am every morning to have his breakfast. He goes to work at 6.30 am. He drives to work on some days. On others, he goes by bus or on a commuter train. He does not leave work until 7.00 in the evening.

- *The block of flats where the Shin family live.*
- *The grass and trees help make this a pleasant suburb of Seoul.*

- *Mr Shin works in an office for the Hyundai Motor Company.*
- *The office is in the central part of Seoul.*
- *He uses computers to help do his work.*

Mrs Shin and her two sons in a local supermarket.

Ye Byong-sook looks after the housework. On some days, she goes to an old people's home to help with the work. She also helps to decorate her local Roman Catholic church for special services. She does most of the shopping in supermarkets near her home.

School and play

Yongsu and Yongsok both go to the same Elementary school. It takes them ten minutes to walk to school. There are 1,650 pupils in the school with about 40 pupils in many of the classes. There is usually homework to do when the boys come home.

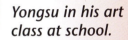

Yongsu in his art class at school.

The boys like to play ball games or roller-skate near the apartment block with their friends. At home, the family play *changi* which is a type of chess, or *yut* which is a board game with sticks and a dice. They also enjoy watching television.

The Shin family sit at a low table for their evening meal.

13

FARMING AND FISHING

Work on farms

In 1970, almost half of South Korea's working population worked in farming and fishing. Now only one in five people work in farming and fishing. There is not much land that can be farmed in South Korea because so much of it is mountainous. It is hard to make a living from farming with only a few small fields.

The farming landscape

Most farms in South Korea are small with only a few hectares of land. The typical farming landscape is a patchwork of small flat fields in a valley bottom, each surrounded by a low earth wall. Many of these are **paddy fields** where rice is grown. Paddy fields have to be **irrigated**, because rice grows in water. Farmers cut narrow steps called **terraces** into the steep valley sides. This gives them more land that they can farm.

Farming and fishing

Although rice is the main crop, farmers also grow many other crops. These include other grain crops, such as barley and maize, and root crops such as taro. Soya beans, cabbage and other vegetables are an important part of South Korean dishes. Mushrooms and different types of herbs are also grown. Ginseng is a herb that is used to make a type of tea. It is also used to make traditional medicines.

Ploughing a field for growing rice.
- *Fields in the valley bottom are small and flat.*
- *It is hard to use the steep valley slopes for farming.*
- *Some farmers still use animals to do the work.*

Fruits, such as apples and water melons, grow well in the warm and moist summers. Farmers rear cattle, pigs and chickens to provide milk, meat and eggs. Most of the food is sent to the cities to be sold. Some farmers rear silk worms for their fine threads of silk. Others grow fields of cotton. These are used to make cloth and clothes in both South Korea and other countries.

South Korean fishermen catch 3.3 million tonnes of fish annually. This makes South Korea the world's number seven country for fishing. Deep-water fishing boats travel to fishing grounds thousands of kilometres away to catch tuna and squid. Just under half the total catch comes from coastal waters near South Korea. Fish are also reared on **fish farms**.

About 45 per cent of all the animal protein eaten by people in South Korea comes from fish.

Fishing trawlers in the port of Sokcho on the east coast of South Korea.
- *Fish is cooked in many South Korean dishes.*
- *South Korea has one of the world's biggest fishing fleets.*

A FISHING FAMILY

- *The Han family outside their home.*
- *The house has one storey and two bedrooms.*

- *Mrs Han waves goodbye to Mr Han as he sets sail.*
- *Mr Han wants to save enough money to buy a bigger boat so he can go further and catch more fish.*

The Han family

Mr and Mrs Han live in a small town called Kampo on the east coast of South Korea. The town is a fishing port with about 9000 people. Mr and Mrs Han live in Kampo with their son Yong-ho. Mr Han's name is Yong-san which means 'longing to live in a high place with enough money'. Mrs Han's name is Ok-hee which means 'a pretty gracious woman like a bead'. Yong-ho means 'standing tall and unshakeable'.

The family live in a small one-storey house made from bricks. There is a garden in front where the Hans grow chrysanthemums and orchids. They also have some miniature pine trees in pots.

A day at sea

Mr Han owns his own fishing boat. On days when he goes fishing, he sails out to sea early in the afternoon. He goes to an area about 20 km away where he knows there are fish. He lowers a net that stays in the water for three days. In the early morning, he pulls up the net he lowered three days ago. He gets back to Kampo at about 6.00 am.

As soon as he lands, he sorts out the fish and drives them to a local market. Buyers bid for the fish then take them away to the cities. Mr Han gets home again in time for breakfast. One favourite meal is a flatfish boiled with red pepper. After breakfast, Mr and Mrs Han go back to the boat to wash it and clean the net. By the afternoon, he is sometimes back on his boat again.

Mrs Han buys some of the food from street traders.

- Mrs Han is getting breakfast ready.
- She is cooking fish and making soup.

Yong-ho's day

Yong-ho goes to the Kampo Middle School. It takes about fifteen minutes to walk there. His best school subjects are English and maths. There are just under 40 children in every class. Yong-ho enjoys the **martial art** of *tae'kwondo*. He is working hard at school so he can go to the police academy and become a police officer.

Yong-ho in his bedroom.

17

MARKETS AND SHOPS

Shopping in the Lotte department store in Seoul.
- *People in South Korea have become wealthy.*
- *They can afford to buy high-cost and high-quality goods.*

Markets for food

For most people in South Korea, their way of life has changed in many ways over the last 30 years. More people now live in towns and cities. City people do not grow their own food or make what they need. They buy their food and other goods in the city shops and markets, like people in any other economically developed country.

Farmers send their food to **wholesale** markets in the cities where it is bought by buyers from shops and restaurants. Seoul is the country's centre for wholesale food markets. Fish from ports all over South Korea are brought to the Noryangjin fish market where they are auctioned to the highest bidders. The 700 stalls are open from early in the morning, so that freshly-caught fish can be bought, sold and eaten on the same day.

A street market.
- *The Southgate market in Seoul.*
- *Visiting a market is a traditional way of shopping in South Korea.*

City shops

Seoul and the other big cities have a wide range of department stores and speciality shops. There are also smart new shopping malls. Most of Seoul's high-quality shops, restaurants and night clubs are in the Myong-dong district. Fashion goods, such as clothes, shoes and jewellery, are some of the goods sold there. Shops away from the centre are mostly small family-run businesses.

Giving good service is an ancient tradition in South Korea. In shops and petrol stations, staff often bow to their customers.

Markets for everything

There are street markets in all the cities. Namdaemun market, near Seoul's city centre, is a market with about 1250 shops and street stalls along every one of its crowded streets. There is not much that cannot be bought there. Things for sale include fresh vegetables, clothes, household goods and craft goods. Some goods are sold directly from the factory, more cheaply than in the shops.

Seoul's Yongsan electronics market is made up of 21 buildings with about 5000 separate shops. They sell all types of electronic goods, including computers, videos, music centres and television sets.

The Kyong-dong market in Seoul is more unusual. It is a centre for selling herbal medicines, such as ginseng and mushrooms.

Athletes visiting South Korea have to be careful when they drink some herbal teas. Herbs such as ginseng can make them fail a drugs test!

19

FOOD

Vegetables and rice

It is said that you can eat as much South Korean food as you like without putting on weight. This is only partly true. The fact is that most South Korean dishes have a lot of vegetables in them and they are not too fattening.

Kimch'i is one example of a vegetable dish that is served with many different types of meals. It is made from fermented vegetables, usually cabbage, mixed with red peppers and garlic. Vegetables are usually seasoned to give them a strong taste. The seasonings include peppers, fermented bean paste called *toenjang*, ginger, garlic and sesame oil.

Rice is part of many South Korean dishes. Cold noodles made from wheat are sometimes eaten in summer. *Pibimpap* is a dish of meat mixed with rice, vegetables, eggs and a red pepper sauce. A soup named *sollongt'ang* is made from rice, beef, sesame seeds and vegetables. A hot chicken soup made with ginseng, garlic, black peppers and rice is supposed to be refreshing on a hot summer's day.

Meat dishes

Meat dishes include *pulgogi* and *kalbi*. In *pulgogi*, thin strips of beef are first soaked in soy sauce, sesame oil and other seasonings, then barbecued over a charcoal grill. *Pulgogi* means 'fire dish'. *Kalbi* is a barbecued dish made with pork.

A street food stall.
- Selling different types of food from a stall in a street market in Seoul.
- Thin slices of vegetables, meat and fish are cooked in the open on a small stove.

A full meal is called a *hanjongshik*. It includes a *kujulp'an* starter course of neatly-arranged strips of vegetables, meats and pancakes. This is followed with meat and fish dishes, together with side plates of vegetables. All the main dishes are put on the table at the same time. People decide for themselves when and how to eat the various dishes. Alcoholic drinks include rice wines and beers.

Eating customs

People eat their meals using chopsticks, although spoons are used for rice and soup. Visitors to South Korea must be careful not to leave their chopsticks in the rice at the end of the meal. Doing this is a sign that somebody has died.

As with every developed country, people in South Korea also eat western foods, such as beefburgers from McDonalds and pizzas from *Pizza Hut*.

It is traditional for people in South Korea to eat meals without talking very much. Burping at the end of the meal is an accepted sign that the meal has been enjoyed.

A family eating breakfast.
- *They sit on the floor at a low table.*
- *Chopsticks and spoons are used to eat the food.*

MADE IN SOUTH KOREA

A world leader

From being almost bottom 30 years ago, South Korea has now become one of the world's leading industrial countries. One South Korean company is the world leader in making computer chips. South Korea is second only to Japan in building ships and second to China in making television sets. South Korea is also in the world's top ten for making tyres, cement, cars and commercial vehicles.

Some of South Korea's biggest companies are known throughout the world. Samsung make music centres, television sets and other electrical goods. Hyundai make ships and cars. Daewoo want to make 2.5 million cars by the year 2000 and sell 1.5 million of them abroad. In South Korea, a big family-owned company is called a *choebal*.

The Hyundai car factory.
- *Welding and some other work on the production line is done by robots.*
- *These methods help keep down manufacturing costs.*
- *Cars are **exported** all over the world.*

A 'Pacific rim' country

South Korea is one of several countries around the '**Pacific rim**' that are called **newly industrialized countries (NICs)**. These countries have become rich by exporting goods that are cheaper to buy than goods made in other industrial countries such as Australia, the UK and the USA.

One key to South Korea's success is good education for its people. Well-educated workers can use high-tech equipment and make new products. Unlike many other Asian countries, South Korea has enough schools, colleges and universities for everyone. One advantage for business is that South Korea's Hangul writing is easier to put onto typewriters and computers than other Asian languages.

The way ahead

At first, factory workers had low pay and poor working conditions. Strikes were against the law. Now workers are paid better, taxed less and work for shorter hours. Since 1987, everyone has been allowed to join a trade union.

However, one problem is that South Korean workers are now paid more than workers in most other Asian countries. Wages in South Korea have gone up by 140 per cent in the last ten years. The result is that some South Korean companies are now employing cheaper workers from Indonesia.

Higher wages have put some South Korean companies out of business. Pusan used to have the world's largest shoe factory, employing 20,000 people. Now it is closed down and all the work is done in Indonesia instead.

In 1996, South Korea held its first international air show. It wants to be a leading country in making aircraft and aircraft equipment by the year 2000. If people in South Korea want to do something, they do their best to make it happen.

The Samsung electronics factory near Seoul.
- *Women do much of the delicate assembly work.*
- *Samsung is one of the world's leading makers of electrical consumer goods.*

TRANSPORT

Spending on transport

In South Korea there is every method of transport that a modern industrial country needs. A network of main roads links all the main cities. The government has just spent $US 52 billion on building more new roads, including a 353 km expressway and 160 km of motorways. These are needed so that people and goods can travel quickly between different parts of the country. In business, time costs money.

Travel in the cities in South Korea is like travel in any other busy modern city. Roads are congested with cars, lorries and buses. There are suburban trains and a subway system in Seoul. Special commuter buses bring workers into the city centre. For the moment, traffic congestion and pollution is the price that people must pay for more wealth.

Travel in central Seoul.
- Buses, cars and bikes crowd the city centre streets of Seoul.
- A haze of pollution is sometimes trapped over the city.

Suburban trains in Seoul.
- *Commuters travel to Taebang station in central Seoul.*
- *Most people depend on public transport to travel about in Seoul.*

The railway network

South Korea has a railway network with just over 3000 km of track covering the whole country. Rail lines link all the main cities and there are high-speed trains between Seoul and Pusan. Good rail links help transport the country's **imported raw materials** to factories. They also carry manufactured goods to the ports, from where they can be **exported**.

Flights and ferries

There is a network of internal air routes between the cities. Seoul's Kimpo airport is one of the world's biggest and busiest with about 73,000 passengers every day. Flights take off and land every two minutes. The demand to travel to and from South Korea is growing so quickly that a new airport is being built. This will be able to handle 270,000 passengers and 920 flights every day.

Most of South Korea's rivers are too shallow, too fast-flowing or too winding to be **navigable**. Small boats can use about 1600 km of inland waterways. There is a steamer service along the south coast between Pusan and Mokpo which is a distance of just over 200 km. There is an eleven-hour sea ferry crossing between Pusan and Cheju Island. This is also a distance of about 200 km. A faster way to travel by sea is to use a hydrofoil service such as the one between Pusan and Yosu.

Respect for old people is shown on crowded buses. Young people stand up so that older people can sit down.

ARTS, LEISURE AND SPORT

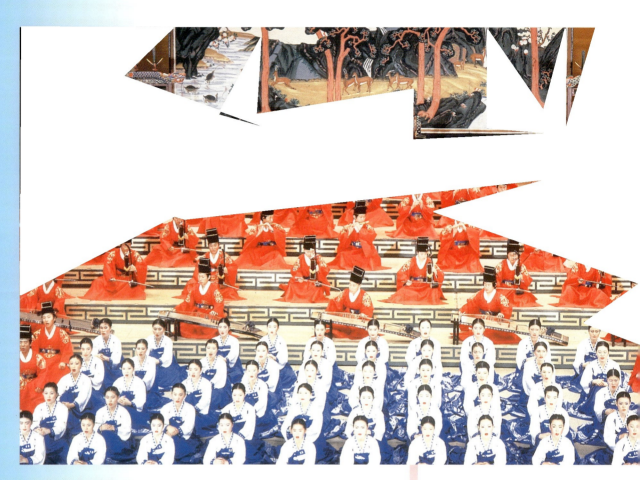

A history of arts

Arts, in various forms, are an important part of South Korea's past and present. Music, dancing and drama were performed in courts and palaces. Farming people performed **folk arts** as part of their work and village life. Folk arts, such as dances with masks and colourful costumes, are still performed in the villages.

There are many traditional musical instruments in South Korea. These include flutes made from bamboo, gongs made from metal, wood and stone, stringed instruments and drums. Formal dancing is often slow and graceful with some movements performed by a dancer balanced on one foot.

Traditional music.
- *A choir and musicians perform ancient court music.*
- *The orchestra includes traditional musical instruments.*

The art of calligraphy, which is a form of handwriting using brushes, is a popular hobby. There is a calligraphy museum in Seoul.

As well as traditional arts, there are also 'western' arts such as ballet and opera. The Seoul Opera House has seats for 2340 people. Modern types of entertainment such as films, television and pop music are as popular with young people in South Korea as in many other countries.

Palaces and parks

As South Koreans become richer, they have more time and money to visit historic palaces and temples. They also enjoy visiting city parks to for a picnic or to go roller-skating. There is open-air ice-skating in winter. The zoo and botanical gardens in Seoul's Children's Park are popular attractions for a day out. Lotte World in Seoul is now the world's biggest indoor theme park. Some people go to the parks for their morning exercises.

The sporting scene

Table tennis and badminton are popular sports. More basketball has been played over the last ten years since there has been a professional basketball league. *Tae'kwondo* is one of South Korea's **martial arts**. Many people also enjoy fishing and watching horse-racing and baseball.

In the year 2002 South Korea and Japan are joint hosts for the football World Cup. This is a way that South Korea can get itself noticed by other countries. It may also help bring more jobs and more wealth.

A survey in 1996 showed that only just over six per cent of South Koreans get the minimum amount of exercise that they ought to have to keep them healthy.

Practising tae'kwondo.
- Tae'kwondo is South Korea's martial arts sport.
- The word tae'kwondo means foot, fist and way.

CUSTOMS AND FESTIVALS

What Confucius said

Many of South Korea's social customs come from the teachings of Confucius who lived in China during the sixth century BC. Confucius taught people how to respect each other. He taught that the ruler is in charge and people must obey the ruler. Wives must be obedient to husbands. Children must be loyal and obedient to parents, then look after them when they grow old. People in South Korea show their respect by bowing to each other.

Buddhism is the country's main religion with about twelve million followers. There are Buddhist temples and shrines, where people come to pray. Some prayers are made to mountain spirits that are said to bring good luck. There are just over ten million Christians, who celebrate Christmas and other Christian festivals.

*A **Confucian** ceremony.*
- *This is being held at a shrine in Seoul.*
- *The teachings of Confucius are still important to people in South Korea.*

Traditional folk dancing.
- *Dances by village people are more lively than court dances.*
- *The dances celebrate social events and special times in the farming year.*
- *Sometimes there are competitions between villages.*

Local festivals

Local festivals are often to do with farming and important events in people's lives, such as birth, marriage and death. In South Korea, people know who their ancestors were, going back for hundreds of years.

Many festivals are held at times when the moon is in a special position. On the fifteenth day after the year's first full moon, village people play games such as tug-of-war. Each team of about 100 people makes a rope from straw, then pulls against the other team. The result of the competition is a sign, telling if the harvest will be good or bad. The most important festival is Sol when the new year is celebrated. The harvest festival is on the fifteenth day of the eighth moon, in September or October.

Love of the past

South Koreans are very proud of their past. Annual festivals are held to celebrate local battles and stories to do with their ancient rulers. For example, the Chongmyo-Taeje royal ceremonies celebrate the kings and queens of the ancient Chosun **dynasty**. The Unnhyon palace in Unni-dong Chongno-gu was restored in 1996. An ancient ceremony has now been revived to celebrate a historic royal wedding.

There are national holidays to celebrate events such as Independence Day, Children's Day and the birthday of the Buddha. These are times when the people can remind themselves of their political and their religious past.

The traditional South Korean calendar is divided into lunar months. These show different phases of the moon. The calendar in the West is a solar calendar that shows the time it takes for the earth to move around the sun. The solar calendar is now also used in South Korea.

SOUTH KOREA FACTFILE

Area 99,173 square kilometres

Highest point Hallasan 1950 m

Climate

	January temp.	July temp.	Total annual rainfall
Seoul	−5 °C	24 °C	1258 mm

Population 45 million

Population density 454 people per square kilometre

Life expectancy female 73, male 67

Capital city Seoul

Population in towns and cities 77%

Population of the main cities (millions)
Seoul 10.6
Pusan 3.8
Taegu 2.2
Inchon 1.8
Kwangju 1.1
Taejon 1.1
Chojun 0.5

Land use
Forest 65%
Crops 19%
Grass 1%
Other 15%

Employment
Services 47%
Industry 36%
Farming 17%

Main imports
Crude oil
Electrical goods
Chemicals
Machinery
Food

Main exports
Cars and ships
Electrical products
Clothes and shoes
Iron and steel
Fish

Language Korean 100%

Religions
Of those who follow religions:
Buddhism 49%
Christian 47%
Confucianism 3%
Other 1%

Money The South Korean won (W)

Wealth $US7660
Note: This is calculated as the total value of what is produced by a country in one year, divided by the population and converted into US dollars.

GLOSSARY

capital city the city where a country has its government

capitalist democracy a political system where people vote for different political ideas and where they can create wealth by owning property and businesses

communism a political system in which everyone is expected to work for the good of everyone else

Confucian to do with the set of beliefs taught by Confucius about how people should behave towards each other

demilitarized zone (DMZ) an area where weapons are not allowed

dynasty a royal family

economically developing country (EDC) a country where many people are poor and where farming and industry are being improved

exported sent out of a country to be sold abroad

fish farms places where fish are reared in tanks to sell

folk arts types of arts and entertainment by ordinary people

imported brought into a country

irrigate to channel water to crops

market towns towns where there are regular markets to buy and sell goods

martial arts ways of defending yourself and training your mind

metro an underground railway

monsoon a seasonal change in the main wind direction

native something which is natural to an area and has always been there

navigable a navigable river is one that boats can use

newly industrialized countries (NICs) countries that have had recent rapid industrial development and become wealthy and successful

Pacific rim countries bordering the Pacific Ocean

paddy fields flooded fields for growing rice

peninsula a narrow neck of land that juts out into the sea

plates very large slabs of the earth's crust

raw materials what goods are made from

sources places where rivers begin to flow

terraces narrow steps of land cut into a hillside for use as fields

third world a term that was used to describe the world's poorest countries

tidal range the difference in height between high and low tide

typhoons the name given to hurricanes in Asia

wholesale selling large amounts of goods at a market to people who intend to sell them on in smaller quantities

INDEX

calligraphy 27
Cheju Island 6, 25
Cheju Strait 6
Chindot-kae dog 9
choebal 22
Chonggyech'on (river) 10
Chosun dynasty 10, 29
Confucius 28

demilitarized zone (DMZ) 5

earthquakes 7

fish farms 15
folk arts 26

gingseng 14, 19, 20

Hallasan 7
Han (river) 7, 13
Hangang (river) 10
Hangul writing 23

irrigated 14

Kampo 16, 17
Kayasan National Park 8
Kimpo airport 25
Korea Strait 7
Kyongbok palace 10
Kyongju 10

market towns 11
martial arts 27
metro 11
Mokopo 25
monsoon 8
Mount Sorak National Park 9
mugunghwa flower 9
myondang 10
Myong-dong 19

Nantkong (river) 7
newly industrialized countries 23

'Pacific rim' 23
paddy fields 14
Pukan (river) 7, 8
Pusan 7, 11, 23, 25

Sea of Japan 6, 7
Seoul 4, 7, 8, 10, 11, 12, 18, 23, 24, 25
Seoul Opera House 27
Shilla dynasty 10
silk worms 15
Sokcho 15
Sorak mountains 6
Ssang-chon river 6

tae'kwondo 27
Taebaek mountains 7
terraces 14
tidal range 6
Toksugung Palace 4
typhoons 8

Ulsan 11
Unnhyon palace 29

wholesale markets 18

Yellow Sea 6
yin and yang 5
Yosu 25